The Significance of Moths

The Significance of Moths

Shirley Camia

TURNSTONE PRESS

The Significance of Moths
copyright © Shirley Camia 2015

Turnstone Press
Artspace Building
206-100 Arthur Street
Winnipeg, MB
R3B 1H3 Canada
www.TurnstonePress.com

All rights reserved. No part of this book may be reproduced or transmitted in any form or by any means—graphic, electronic or mechanical—without the prior written permission of the publisher. Any request to photocopy any part of this book shall be directed in writing to Access Copyright, Toronto.

Turnstone Press gratefully acknowledges the assistance of the Canada Council for the Arts, the Manitoba Arts Council, the Government of Canada through the Canada Book Fund, and the Province of Manitoba through the Book Publishing Tax Credit and the Book Publisher Marketing Assistance Program.

Printed and bound in Canada by Friesens for Turnstone Press.

Library and Archives Canada Cataloguing in Publication

Camia, Shirley, 1979-, author

    The significance of moths / Shirley Camia.

Poems.

ISBN 978-0-88801-533-4 (pbk.)

    I. Title.

PS8605.A49S54 2015   C811'.6   C2014-907890-0

For Mom and Tatay

Contents

In the Palm of an Evening

Wake / 5
News / 6
Before Sleep / 7
Pan de Sal / 8
Lola / 9
Signs of Age / 10
As One Lay Dying / 11
Cathedral / 12
Thirst / 13

The Portrait Unravelling

The Definition of Home I / 17
Jeepney Ride / 18
Long Drive / 19
To the Old City / 20
Master / 21
As Luck Would Have It / 22
The Daily Ebb and Flow / 23
Labandera / 24

Lost Treasure / 25
The Departure / 26

Humbled Knowing

The New Home / 29
Lunch Special / 30
Longing / 31
Black Widow / 32
Part-time Job / 33
Garment Worker / 34
Needlework / 35
Girls' World / 36
Closing Time / 37
A Life Gleaned in the Eye of a Needle / 38

A Song from the Old Country

Looking Back / 41
What You Can't Take with You / 42
Telephone / 43
Long Distance / 44
Galing sa Abroad / 45
The Definition of Home II / 46
Entitled / 47
Snow Day / 48

Return / 49
Nostalgia / 50

The Generation After

The Generation After / 53
Wishes / 54
Advice / 55
Lessons / 56
You Can't Do That / 57
It's All in the Delivery / 58
Cardinal Beauty / 59
Winter Arrival / 60
Bicycle / 61
Ballet Class / 62
The Invincible One / 63

Straddling Worlds

Spectacle / 67
Forbidden Discussions / 68
Questions / 69
Protecting the Child / 70
Portrait / 71
Fall / 72
Castaway / 73

On the Playground / 74
Taunts / 75
Letters / 76
Seafarer / 77
Memory / 78
The Definition of Home III / 79
Forever Her / 80
An Ending / 81

Glossary and Notes on the Poems / 83
Acknowledgements / 85

The Significance of Moths

In the Palm of an Evening

Wake

brown moths circle like carousels
matching the shade of her linen dress
and the earth to which she is about to return

she'd lived an ordinary life

survived by five children
joining a husband who died long before

her hair in purple ribbons
silk and burnished gold

this woman

a gift to the living
dissolved
in the palm of an evening

News

i was sent away before
they brought *lola*'s body elsewhere

the truth concealed by distance

until its whisper became a roar
that shook the guava trees

even the blossoms shuddered

Before Sleep

it was a soothing ritual
rubbing drops of oil into her palm
smoothing it into her thinning hair

working out the day in knots
released at night
from the choke of *lola*'s comb

i'd watch from the foot of the stairs

strands of the past
bound to the present

tumbling like laughter
gently down her back

Pan de Sal

the loud blasts of *jeepney* horns
rude wails that break the melody
of a meditative morning

merchants pipe in
with harmonies
selling hot breakfast

the sweet smell of salt bread
sails along the soothing breeze

awakens a dreaming *lola*
cloaked in slivers of dawn's glow

Lola

i am the only one
who remembers the kiss
that missed
your face

afraid that death came in particles
a disease we would carry
like *balikbayan* boxes
overseas

but you lived two more years

longer than expected
shorter than the life of that photo
hanging like sorrow

your powdery skin
my reluctant embrace

Signs of Age

the etched lines
on the old woman's face

form a path of searching rivers

solemn and deep
forgetting nothing

As One Lay Dying

there was nothing left but eyes

a glimpse of darkness
reflecting the hospital's
fluorescent light

pleading with death

Cathedral

the place of lost souls and sweat

where incense mingles
with cigarettes

stoked by greying handkerchiefs

blades of fraying spanish lace
cutting the humid air

Thirst

run along the wrinkled earth
as trails of dust awake

the infinite playground

where lush green canopies
once drowned
in swampy fields

now hardened by the years

The Portrait Unravelling

The Definition of Home I

palm tree umbrellas
line rows
of submerged rice fields

the portrait unravelling

under a rooster's
crow

and the lives
of a thousand
memories

Jeepney Ride

hidden behind handkerchiefs
passengers' tough faces
made tougher still
by caked-in soot
settled into the grooves
of life

eyes speak in curiosity

squints and stares
a sustained chord
broken
by an urgent knock
demanding a stop

Long Drive

where shades of green
form a uniform
hue

where rolling meadows
are stabbed
by jagged mass
of sprawling stone

along the highway

wounds peek through bandages
scars in the making

To the Old City

the rain pounds
dissolves
into a tattered mist

spits as it shifts

in the shadow of grey
that rises

into a mountain

Master

the rise of dawn
and a forceful whip
break the backs
of the *carabao*

their power sinks
with hooves in fresh mud

expelled with each draw of breath

at the helm
a darkened boy

scowls at the snarl of mosquitoes

hissing past
his cigarette

As Luck Would Have It

this is one's life by chance

bathing in backed
up sewers

posing as pestilent streams

where the cool
of cement block cells

gives refuge

from the heat
of a concrete coffin
propped on stilts

someone's home

The Daily Ebb and Flow

in my mother's island town
the water used to flow
in and out
of the house each day

an unwanted but expected suitor

splashing charm like cologne
until its attention
unreturned

waned

leaving residual relief
and a surprising sense
of loss

Labandera

there are no secrets at the well

just experiences lived
and forgotten

making way

for a fresh tomorrow
the next tomorrow

Lost Treasure

sounds of the sea bring the hush of old love
memories in seashells
heartache in the wail of the gulls

flotsam that dissolves
with the boom of a ship's call

The Departure

the day was full of years
packed in a broken suitcase

as mama's lip quivered

a violin string
playing a sadness
that rang until hollow

a cry for her old life
and the lives she let go

Humbled Knowing

The New Home

hail the great city
that begins with a win

but ends
in loss

as dreams
like families

splinter

Lunch Special

the shredded remains
of a daily meal

waste
abandoned on its dirty plate

as you flash back

to food stalls by polluted waters
garbage floating upstream

and ten *centavos*

gripped
in your hand

hungry

Longing

row upon row
of seedlings lined
like farmers' crops

bounty pressed
between the pages of stories

harvested for grains
surviving the long sun

Black Widow

velvet is the voice that stings with confession
steals the money in the drawer and is gone

but the blow of anger
bellows and looms

like the wail of an accordion

or the sticky threads of a delicate web
long after the
spider

Part-time Job

you came home that first day
with your uniform pressed

smiling

at the possibilities
it promised

the colour of birch
the scent of lemons

but here now
humbled knowing

cleaning toilets
your road
to distant riches

Garment Worker

eight hours dissolve
into yesterday
this day
and the next

as busy fingers
blank eyes
and stitch after stitch

alter the world

Needlework

how many tales
are knit into
that honeycombed fortress
born from the twisting
of string and fluid hands

as one sits quiet
wishing

Girls' World

i nearly cut
my finger once

on a ferocious fang
piercing
a denim skin

among a chorus of seams

an angry gasp
from a sputtering machine

Closing Time

a break in the whir of the machines

enough time to wipe off
the day's threads

ends that collect under
creaky wooden floorboards

before the whistle blows

A Life Gleaned in the Eye of a Needle

steady those shaky hands
whose tremors
cut the air
like the heads
of bobbing needles

their power once hinged

on the beast
that did
them in

A Song from the Old Country

Looking Back

was it a regret coming to a place like this

without the smell of *sampaguita* carried over
by a sweeping tide

without the boisterous jostling of children
climbing aboard those rickety boats

seizing dinner
seizing survival

tell me

when you look
at your angry worn hands

was it

What You Can't Take with You

do you remember the reeds that closed in
before they opened up to a world engulfed
by the blues of the sky and sea

a world where men whose faces
cracked like roasted pig skin
sent out smoky circles
cut by children chasing chickens

flies swirled in a cyclone
as the gulls swooped in

do you remember

a world before the rains
before the petals fell

one by one

Telephone

a ring shoots the night like a pistol
launching fear deep into the house

insistent tones
echo within echoes

is this the same news from last month

news of the hungry
news of the cold

Long Distance

what really speaks
through telephone lines

cut by crackles
and the noisy buzz

of distance

the message found
in huffs of breath
and moody sighs

Galing sa Abroad

how does it feel
to have no connection
to the place you call
home

where you're met with open palms
not arms
that rattle and nag at your guilt

dig deep into your pockets
for (this will not) change

The Definition of Home II

the long droughts of winter
are thawed in the memories

of an island

surrounded by filthy water
and guards with guns

Entitled

there are no secrets
on an island
sometimes swallowed by the sea

where bloodlines
live like beggars
hoarding a feast

earned
from others' labour

their only poverty pride

Snow Day

summer returns
in the scent
of a lemon

laundry tossed
on a flailing line

sun-warmed cotton
hung as flags
pleading surrender

Return

turn back
to the tall grass

that is home

where searing summers
mark a rebirth

a warm nuzzle
consoling heartbreak

Nostalgia

in the quiet explosion of sunrise
a single flute
rises
over the rush of the crowd

a song from the old country

reminding them
how far
they have come

The Generation After

The Generation After

in between
canola fields
and surf

a suspension bridge lies

tethered

by
achievement
and
accolades

burdened
by the eyes
of expectation

Wishes

the dress was a violent pink
the colour of hope
of a daughter's rising
over the stink

at the stall by the butcher

where dreams
in hard currency
are sold

Advice

transcend the confines of your birth
cut through the thicket
of deeply threaded vines

defy the devil's dirge

seductive
damning
calling

Lessons

these chords will always fall flat
broken as they unfold
music empty of warmth
a razor slicing the keys

an unwritten song
unable to stand

You Can't Do That

often limitations are spoken
before an infinite silence

an absolute born of poverty
that cannot be explained

to a child

steady pride
the mask
for a vast longing

It's All in the Delivery

the bad news lies
not in shrill words
that cut the air
like winter breath

but soft honeyed sounds

tricking teasing tickling
the ear

carefree as paper planes

Cardinal Beauty

a splash of red
flees
the desperate clutch
of deadened trees

a matador's flag
for the bull
of winter

Winter Arrival

pocketfuls of snow
dust the soil
like icing sugar on
chiffon cakes
that celebrated
each birthday

orange rind
peeled and grated

a memory rising

Bicycle

it wasn't a birthday
but a present
nonetheless
rolled up to school

heads turned and eyes stared

shiny and wide
as the tires of a new bike

its streamers ferried truths
into the distance
its chrome gleamed
blinding
like a parent's love

Ballet Class

they walked into
a box of jelly beans

scrambled sweets in a frenzied twirl

cotton candy pinwheels
tufts of taffeta unfurled

their daughter

bowing to the grace of the ribbons

The Invincible One

he was the baby of the family
who ran past bungalows
lined in neat rows
like sprouting crops

shrouded under elms
bowing their heads in salute

to the fury of his step

Straddling Worlds

Spectacle

we left the circus early
as flushed children waited on the
elephants eating peanuts

handfuls thrown at the reaching trunks
backs drooped with captivity and the
tugging insistence of unbridled riders

they think elephants are animals
whispered a disapproving voice
but i didn't turn to look

my gaze fixed on the shrinking crush of colour
i left tightly reined
like the elephants in their tasselled robes

Forbidden Discussions

the memory
etched on our tongues
has no voice

its tastes and colours
banned and branded
like cattle off to slaughter

resigned to hissed whispers
a humbling song

our broken grace

Questions

there is so much that i want to know

about the father who died
prematurely after troubling
the *duwende* who made
his belly bloat
to a yellow balloon
cutting his life short
reduced to a memory
and a searing pain
felt by *lola* when she
touched her abdomen
staring at five children
with hungry mouths
gaping mouths
empty mouths

but i don't know how to ask

Protecting the Child

the boxes bore *lola*'s name
on all sides
destined for back home

kept secret for months

distant shores
described
as trips to the store

but i knew

our separation
forever

Portrait

my father
whose face
punctuated with the same
worked in lines of his glove

moves summer slow

deliberate like the slope of a mountain
at home winding up for a pitch

Fall

drops of yellow
droop like stained rags

leaves
that eventually
scatter

cleared
by a father's hands

Castaway

father and daughter
side by side
solemn as statues
bronzed on the deck

their moods compressed
to a bullet-shaped weight

flung to the water

hobbling
sinking

On the Playground

a string of barbs circles overhead

as a wreath of birds
dives in

feasts

on tiny vulnerabilities

Taunts

by the old portuguese fish store
sounds as rotten as the smell

pounding her pride
and jellyfish spine

kids on bikes
telling her where to go

because of her skin

Letters

a boundless sea of words
weights the wings of a paper crane

with the soaring hopes of childhood

set free

in the folds
of a note

Seafarer

he was never there
but the letters would tell you otherwise
charismatic loops that formed words
on stamped pages
pressed like carvings knifed on wooden desks

or pictures with corners bent
like ears inward
weary of the history they tell

a ghost that lives in scattered exchanges
looms in parcels delivered in the mail

Memory

deeds and demons
mark their presence
like frost on a window

cold drips of ink slips
come as flurries

storm the page

gleaming calm
a moment after

The Definition of Home III

the pots brim with history
in mama's kitchen

recollections boil
as the skillets hiss their aversion

a warm coat of traditions
textures and tastes

Forever Her

the girl from dominion
who grew up
in the shadow
of a plum tree

in the shadow still

the girl from dominion

straddling
worlds

An Ending

the dance of the moth is over
its antennae drumming with broken fury
until the body gasps
and lies still

silence arrives
to the wings
in unflight

a power
already forgotten

Glossary & Notes on the Poems

Balikbayan—Literally, "returning to country" in Tagalog, a *balikbayan* is a Filipino who returns to the Philippines after a lengthy period of time away. *Balikbayan* boxes, meanwhile, are large cardboard boxes filled with gifts, often clothing and daily household items such as soap and non-perishable food items, that are sent by Filipinos living overseas to their families and friends back home. Found in: "*Lola*"

Carabao—Also known as the Asian water buffalo, a *carabao* is a mammal that is very common in the Philippines. It's considered to be the country's national animal. Found in: "Master"

Centavos—*Centavos* are the coins of the Philippine peso, in the same way cents are to the dollar. Ten *centavos* are worth one-tenth of a peso. Found in: "Lunch Special"

Duwende—A *duwende* is a sprite or dwarf in Filipino mythology. As my mother told me, they are found in many places, including dark parts of homes. They can be evil if they feel that their territory is being disturbed, so one must tread carefully if a *duwende* is suspected nearby. Found in: "Questions"

Galing sa Abroad—Literally, "came from abroad" in Tagalog. The term can be used negatively to describe someone who is now viewed as arrogant because they have been overseas. Found in: "*Galing sa Abroad*"

Jeepney—A *jeepney* is a mode of public transport in the Philippines. It is very distinctive, often decorated with bright colours and designs. They were originally former military vehicles used by the US Army in WWII. Found in: "*Pan de Sal*" and "*Jeepney* Ride"

Labandera—A Tagalog word, a *labandera* is someone, usually a woman, who does laundry. Found in: "*Labandera*"

Lola—From the Spanish word *abuela*, *lola* means grandmother. Found in: "News," "Before Sleep," "*Pan de Sal*," "*Lola*," "Questions" and "Protecting the Child"

Long Drive—The Filipino equivalent of "road trip," "long drive" is a term that is commonly used by Filipinos when referring to driving trips, i.e., "We're going on a long drive." The poem is my homage to some of the sights seen during a long drive, as people travel to a new destination. Found in: "Long Drive"

Pan de Sal—"Salt bread" in Spanish, *pan de sal* is a bread roll that, despite the literal translation of its name, is actually sweet. *Pan de sal* is often served at breakfast. Found in: "*Pan de Sal*"

Sampaguita—The *sampaguita* is a small, white and sweet-smelling flower that is part of the jasmine family. It is the national flower of the Philippines. Found in: "Looking Back"

Acknowledgements

I have many people to thank for helping bring these poems to light:

Thank you to my parents, for allowing me to write, for buying books that allowed me to fall in love with words and for constantly allowing me to invade their private lives as I mined the past for poems.

Thank you to my large extended family for the company and the endless laughter.

Thank you to Andy Bernstein for believing in my work.

Thank you to the Singer/Gelineaus and the Bernstein/Breitmans for your support.

Thank you to Jamis, Sharon and Michelle, my heroes at Turnstone Press, for your unwavering enthusiasm.

Thank you to Robert Joseph for always lending a critical eye.

Thank you to the Ontario Arts Council for helping fund the creation of this book.

Thank you to everyone who has supported me in various ways, from purchasing my work to providing a free meal to kind words in times requiring patience and grace.